Stand By Me

Susan

God Bless!

Mark Draughty

Also by Dave and Jan Dravecky

Resources by Dave Dravecky
Comeback (with Tim Stafford)
When You Can't Come Back (with Ken Gire)
The Worth of a Man (with C. W. Neal)
The Worth of a Man (audio)

Resources by Jan Dravecky
A Joy I'd Never Known (with Connie Neal)
A Joy I'd Never Known (audio)

Resources by Dave and Jan Dravecky
Do Not Lose Heart (with Steve Halliday)
Stand by Me (with Amanda Sorenson)

Stand By Me

A Guidebook of Practical Ways to Encourage a Hurting Friend

DAVE & JAN DRAVECKY WITH AMANDA SORENSON

ZondervanPublishingHouse

Grand Rapids, Michigan

A Division of HarperCollinsPublishers

Stand by Me
Copyright © 1998 by David and Janice Dravecky

Requests for information should be addressed to:
📖 ZondervanPublishingHouse
Grand Rapids, Michigan 49530

Library of Congress Cataloging-in-Publication Data
Stand by me : a guidebook of practical ways to encourage a hurting friend /
  [compiled by] Dave and Jan Dravecky with Amanda Sorenson.
      p.   cm.
  ISBN 0-310-21646-X (softcover)
    1. Encouragement—Religious aspects—Christianity—Quotations, maxims,
etc.   2. Friendship—Religious aspects—Christianity—Quotations, maxims,
etc.   I. Dravecky, Dave.   II. Dravecky, Jan.   III. Sorenson, Amanda, 1953–   .
BV4647.E53S73   1998
242'.4—dc21   98–10281
                                                                         CIP

All Scripture quotations, unless otherwise indicated, are taken from the *Holy Bible:
New International Version*®. NIV®. Copyright © 1973, 1978, 1984 by International
Bible Society. Used by permission of Zondervan Publishing House. All rights
reserved.

Published in association with the literary agency of Alive Communications, Inc.,
1465 Kelly Johnson Blvd. #320, Colorado Springs, CO 80920

Interior design by Jody DeNeef

Printed in the United States of America

98 99 00 01 02 03 04 /❖ DC/ 10 9 8 7 6 5 4 3 2

DEDICATED TO:

THE STAFF AT THE OUTREACH OF HOPE

*He who refreshes others will
himself be refreshed*

PROVERBS 11:25

Contents

INTRODUCTION

When we know someone who is hurting, many of us want to help, but often we do nothing. Why?

Some of us are scared. And for good reason. Comforting those who hurt is difficult and unfamiliar ground for most of us.

Others of us think we don't have the time. Yes, it takes time to reach out to another person, but encouragement can come in surprisingly small packages.

Most of us feel inadequate, that we can't do enough. And we are inadequate to completely meet the needs of those who suffer. But that doesn't mean we can't take away some of the pain.

Most of us think we have to say something in order to comfort, and we don't know what to say. But words are not the key to encouragement. In order to minister to a hurting person in words, we usually need to *know* that person well. Most of the time we won't have the deep, abiding relationship that enables us to minister through what we say, but there are hundreds of other ways we can encourage one another.

Scripture tells us the way of encouragement that will never fail: "Dear children, let us not love with words or tongue but with actions and in truth" (1 John 3:18). Our desire is to take you on a journey of encouragement. Some friends of ours who know the meaning of suffering will accompany us through the pages of this book. Together we want to help you discover the actions you can take to help encourage and comfort someone who is suffering.

DAVE AND JAN DRAVECKY

FRIENDS

ARE

MOTIVATED

BY

LOVE

How to become an encourager? Begin by going to God, who is your encourager, and asking Him to soften your heart and infuse you with love and concern for others. . . . Put yourself in the other person's shoes: spend a few moments thinking about the concerns in that person's life.

LOIS MOWDAY RABEY

If I speak in the tongues of men and of angels, but have not love, I am only a resounding gong or a clanging cymbal. . . . If I give all . . . but have not love, I gain nothing. . . . Love never fails.

1 CORINTHIANS 13:3, 8

There is no substitute for sincere love when reaching out to those who suffer. One cancer survivor says, "I hated being an 'assignment' for some people."

Fragile and delicate are the feelings of most who seek our help. They need to sense we are there because we care . . . not just because it's our job.

CHARLES SWINDOLL

Love is not enough; it has to be love with action. Love enough to carry a piece of my pain and share my hurt.

DAVE BIEBEL

He who knows he is loved can be content with a piece of bread, while all the luxuries of the world cannot satisfy the craving of the lonely.

FRANCES J. ROBERTS

A FRIEND
SHARES
A MOST
PRECIOUS
GIFT —
THE GIFT
OF SELF

It meant so much for friends to come and just sit with us or listen to us if we needed to talk or cry. To know that someone had cleared a busy schedule to come to our side to be with us . . . was the most tangible display of "denying self" that we witnessed.

CANDY COOPER

Yes, at times encouraging a hurting friend is difficult—even painful. But the sacrifice I make in the process of encouraging is far less than the pain my suffering friend endures.

KIM JONES

Jan and I received encouragement in many different ways. Often it came in the form of letters, cards, and gifts from people we didn't even know. That encouragement is wonderful, but we were also deeply blessed by people close to us who encouraged us by what they gave of themselves.

I think of our friends Bobby and Patty. She was scared to death of flying, but she stepped way out of her "comfort zone" and got on an airplane with her husband just to be with me during one of my surgeries. That is a gift of one's self.

During one of my hospitalizations, my team was in New York for a game. Several of my teammates took the time to come and see me. There were plenty of other things they could have done with their time, but they came to see me. It was so good to look up and see their faces in my hospital room.

And I think of my friend Sealy Yates who took time out of his incredibly busy schedule and spent several days by my side. He listened when I wanted to talk and did whatever I needed him to do, twenty-four hours a day. He even slept on an uncomfortable cot next to my hospital bed. It was such a comfort to awaken in the middle of the night and see that I wasn't alone. To this day, the sacrifice he made blows me away.

DAVE DRAVECKY

Being an encourager is costly. It takes thought, time, and energy. Most of us live such frantic, self-centered lives that we simply don't notice other people's need for encouragement. We're so busy keeping up with our own lives that we don't take time to stop and think how we might touch someone else.

LOIS MOWDAY RABEY

My command is this: Love each other as I have loved you. Greater love has no one than this, that he lay down his life for his friends.

JOHN 15:12-13

$\mathcal{A}$NYONE—

A STRANGER,

A CHILD,

A CLOWN—

CAN BE

A FRIEND

$\mathcal{A}$ man selected some sheet music and carried it to the cash register in a Christian bookstore. "Do you sing or play?" the sales clerk asked cheerily.

"I sing," he answered, "but this is for my nephew who will sing at my wife's funeral." Then he started to cry.

The clerk quietly closed the register, then held his hand until he regained his composure. "Afterward," she said, "he thanked me—just for that."

CBA *FRONTLINE*

$\mathcal{W}$e each have the power to be an encouragement to someone.

ROSEMARY COOPER

One day I delivered a balloon bouquet to the home of a young cancer patient. I was dressed in my clown suit and did not plan to go into the home because the boy was afraid of clowns. But when I got to the door, his younger sister went racing into his room full of excitement, shouting, "There's a clown here! There's a clown!"

Surprisingly, the boy wanted to see me, so I went into his room. I was not prepared for what I saw—for how swollen he was—but I prayed and started talking with him. I wanted to make a balloon animal for him, so I blew up a balloon on my little compressor. Just as it was about full, it popped off and— P-F-F-F-F-T!—went flying across the room! This had never happened to me before, so it startled me, and the little boy started laughing. Before we were finished, the balloon flew off the compressor three times! That little boy laughed and laughed and laughed.

When I left his room, I prayed with his mother. She cried. I knew that little boy hadn't laughed like that for a long time. If God can use a silly clown to encourage someone, surely He can use you.

PRISSILLY THE CLOWN

Several times during our son's illness, we received a card, a movie rental coupon, a dinner certificate, a book, or a plaque from someone who simply wanted to be known as "The Lord's Servant." To this day I don't know who that person was, but I am grateful that God placed our needs on his or her heart.

CANDY COOPER

And there are different ways that God works in people; but all these ways are from the same God. God works in us all in everything we do.

1 CORINTHIANS 12:6 (icb)

My daughter's stylist was an encourager. He gently shaved off her remaining strings of hair. He talked openly with us about her new "hair style." He was an answered prayer.

ROSEMARY COOPER

My brother, you have shown love to God's people. You have made them feel happy. This has given me great joy and comfort.

PHILEMON 7 (icb)

Our son's teenage baby-sitter became good friends with him during his illness. He kept her picture by his bed. On one of his last mornings with us, she and her sister brought him cookies that they had baked. He never felt like eating them, but I know he appreciated what they did.

CANDY COOPER

Contrary to what you may believe, you don't have to endure some disaster before you can bring a touch of God's grace to a friend.

DAVE BIEBEL

The many letters I have received from kids have been a great encouragement to me. I once received a letter from a boy who stuck his arm inside his shirt so he looked like he didn't have an arm. He then walked around a mall, "just so I could know how you feel."

DAVE DRAVECKY

Something from the Spirit can be seen in each person, to help everyone

1 CORINTHIANS 12:7(icb)

A

FRIEND

WALKS

BESIDE

YOU

The cards that included a personal note such as expressions of grieving with us, agonizing with us, or standing in faith with us, let us know that we weren't alone in our struggle.

CANDY COOPER

God hurts when we hurt. When you ache with your broken-hearted friend, you emulate the heart of God.

DAVE BIEBEL

Just a few months after my amputation, I needed to fulfill a speaking commitment at a three-day conference in another state. I was at a very low point physically and emotionally and truly didn't have the strength to do what I had been asked to do. That's when my friend, Atlee Hammaker, stepped in to walk beside me. He left his home for several days just to be with me in that distant city. We shared a great time together, and his presence helped me focus on the task at hand and accomplish it.

DAVE DRAVECKY

I sought my soul,
But my soul I could not see.
I sought my God,
But my God eluded me.
I sought my brother,
And I found all three.

AUTHOR UNKNOWN

$\mathcal{I}$ especially appreciated the friends who came to sit with me during Dave's surgeries. One particular friend could accept me in whatever state I was in. I could be really ugly—angry, doubtful, fearful—with her, and she remained beside me and loved me.

JAN DRAVECKY

$\mathcal{B}$eing there when your friend needs someone to share the pain is the most important factor in being a mender of hearts.

DAVE BIEBEL

When both Dave and I were at our lowest point, Dave's parents moved in with us and gave us eight weeks of their lives to care for us and our children. We needed that because at the time we couldn't do it ourselves.

JAN DRAVECKY

Two are better than one, because they have a good return for their work: If one falls down, his friend can help him up. But pity the man who falls and has no one to help him up!

ECCLESIASTES 4:9-10

Support groups for specific medical conditions can be a great source of encouragement, but when a person is weak, sick, or in pain, it can be frightening to venture out into the company of strangers. Find out what support groups are available for your friend, and offer to accompany your friend to the first few meetings.

As you journey with your friend ... you can go together where neither of you would have the security to go alone, because what you are together is more than either of you could possibly be alone.

DAVE BIEBEL

Write down your friend's medical appointments on your personal planner or calendar. Then call to see how the visit went. Be the friend who shares the anxiety of these visits.

KIM JONES

A friend is one who joyfully sings with you when you are on the mountain top and silently walks beside you through the valley.

WILLIAM A. WARD

People make sterile hospital rooms a little more bearable. It means so much to have someone by your side to soften harsh treatments and make lengthy hospital stays pass more quickly.

BRIAN NEWHOUSE

A friend loves you all the time. A brother is always there to help you.

PROVERBS 17:17 (icb)

A FRIEND IS

NOT AFRAID

TO SHARE

YOUR TEARS

OR PAIN

Praise be to the God and Father of our Lord Jesus Christ, the Father of compassion and the God of all comfort, who comforts us in all our troubles, so that we can comfort those in any trouble with the comfort we ourselves have received from God. For just as the sufferings of Christ flow over into our lives, so also through Christ our comfort overflows. . . . And our hope for you is firm, because we know that just as you share in our sufferings, so also you share in our comfort.

2 CORINTHIANS 1:3–7

Those special servants of God who extend mercy to the miserable often do so with much encouragement because they identify with the sorrowing—they get "inside their skin." Rather than watching from a distance or keeping the needy safely at arm's length, they get in touch, involved, and offer assistance that alleviates some of the pain.

CHARLES SWINDOLL

. . . An Encourager, one who puts courage into the faint-hearted, one who nerves the feeble arm for fight, one who makes a very ordinary man cope gallantly with a perilous and a dangerous situation.

WILLIAM BARCLAY

If we want to encourage people . . . we must not start from the presupposition that Christians should not grieve, that Christians should not feel pain, that Christians should not suffer great trials or that Christians should not become deeply discouraged. Not only is this unrealistic on our part, it is unbiblical. If we begin with these presuppositions, we come as "Job encouragers."

DAVID JEREMIAH

Stifle all your aspirations but one—to be an agent of grace in the midst of your friend's pain.

DAVE BIEBEL

My best friend and I had been friends for thirty-five years when her youngest son took his life. After his funeral, some of his friends—one of whom was my son—stood around his grave and sang his favorite hymns. At the time I thought, *Oh Lord, the pain she must be feeling. How does one bear the pain of losing a child?* I couldn't in a million years imagine losing my son, my only child. But three years later, I lost him to cancer.

Now I, too, know the pain of losing a child. I share all the pain my friend felt. She is always there for me, like a sister. When I can't see through my pain and sorrow, I call her. We cry. Oh, do we cry. She prays with me on the phone. Together we pray for strength for ourselves and for our families. Together we hold close to our hearts the promise that we will be reunited with our boys some day.

SARA HINES

People we knew did not know what to say or do, so they backed away. We walked in a world that was either "blind" to what we were experiencing, "helpless" to act in an encouraging way, or plainly did not care. I turned to more than daily prayer. I literally prayed in my rising up, in my lying down, in the middle of the night. I talked to God when I was sure that no one wanted to hear any more. I'm not sure even God would want me to talk to Him that often!

ROSEMARY COOPER

A friend is one who walks in when the rest of the world walks out.

Discouraged people don't need critics. They hurt enough already. They don't need more guilt or piled-on distress. They need encouragement. They need a refuge. A place to hide and heal.

CHARLES SWINDOLL

A true friend is someone who is faithful in little things. A true friend is not afraid to take the risk of loving, even when it seems difficult. A true friend is not afraid to feel the pain of others.

HEATHER GROUNDS

ENCOURAGEMENT

MAKES A

DIFFERENCE—

EVEN

WHEN IT'S

IN SMALL

DOSES

So many friends left encouraging messages on our answering machine. Some of them we recorded and played back to our son while he was in the hospital.

SARA HINES

Therefore encourage one another and build each other up, just as in fact you are doing.

1 THESSALONIANS 5:11

The little gifts of thoughtfulness that make a difference . . .

- The notecards and stamps for thank-yous.
- The month of prepaid parking at the hospital.
- The quarters for phone calls.
- The long-distance phone card that makes it easy to keep in touch with family.
- The favorite candy bar or snack food.
- The encouraging card that includes twenty dollars for a surprise pizza party.
- The sack of groceries left on the front porch.
- The subscription to a favorite magazine.
- The tokens or ticket books for the tolls one must pay to get to and from treatments.
- The hospital cafeteria gift certificate.

To God there are no small offerings if they are made in the name of His Son.

A. W. TOZER

During hospitalization for my first surgery, neither my room-mate nor I could walk, and our night nurse took extra care to make our stay more pleasant. My roommate and I would watch the World Series on television at night, and our nurse went out of her way to bring us after-hours snacks during the game. We loved it. Whether she brought us cherry Italian ices or hot water for instant soup, she turned what could have been a boring evening into a special event.

DAVE DRAVECKY

Encouragement is oxygen to the soul. No one ever lived without it.
GEORGE MATTHEW ADAMS

During his last months of life, there were times when my son was so ill that I would not leave his side. I was so grateful for the times his nurses cared enough to go beyond the call of duty and bring lunch to me.

SARA HINES

If you think you are too small to be effective, you have never been in bed with a mosquito.

BETTY REESE

A

FRIEND

IS

FAITHFUL

Seems like you know when I need you
　　Seems like He knows who to send
　　You never come as a prophet
　　Just an open hearted friend . . .
　　Some days I feel like a failure
　　And I'd love to leave it all
　　I see no reason to go on
　　That's when you decide to call
　　Making it simple and clear
　　That's why your voice is so dear
　　My heart takes courage from hearing you say
　　You are a true friend . . . .

TWILA PARIS

One neighbor calls every week to "check" on us. She prays every day for us. She has learned what is really happening in our family. Not only does she pray, but she regularly tells me she prays and sometimes sends me a note to remind me that she is praying. Such a faithful encourager is truly a gift from God.

ROSEMARY COOPER

Friendship is one of the sweetest joys of life. Many might have failed beneath the bitterness of their trial had they not found a friend.

CHARLES HADDON SPURGEON

Take a commitment to do something—take a walk, play golf or tennis, go out to eat at a nice restaurant, attend a concert, or see a movie— once a month with a friend whose spouse is dealing with a long-term infirmity. Make sure you follow through! At a time when most friends scatter, the support of a faithful friend becomes even more precious. This is also good to do for at least a year following the death of a loved one.

God really promises, "do not fear, for I am with you." But it can be nearly impossible for a hurting person to believe this until someone comes alongside to "make God visible."

DAVE BIEBEL

One special friend, a cancer survivor and mother of grown children, was my constant source of human encouragement and hope. She let my children spend the night at her house when we were at the hospital, bought them presents, let them swim in her pool. She listened to me cry umpteen times and allowed me to pour out my despairing heart without restraint or conditions. She faithfully prayed for me and with me, always pointing me toward the loving arms of Jesus.

The night before our son died, I called her just as she was walking out the door to go to church. At my request, she put aside her plans and came to be with us, to be available for whatever we needed. My husband and older children were at church, and I was afraid. Deep inside I think I knew Adam was dying, and I didn't want to be alone. She spent the entire evening with us. Adam really loved "Miss Camille." When I left his room to attend to his younger sister, she sat with him and prayed. Later she told me that it was one of the most incredible nights of her life. She felt the presence of God in our home that night and witnessed firsthand God's preparation of coming for Adam.

CANDY COOPER

People in need often hear the words, "Call if you need anything." But more often than not, people who are the most needy either don't know or can't express what they need or want. Even when they know what they need, they may be unable to take the initiative to call. So it is important for a friend to take the initiative to keep in touch and offer tangible support.

The ministry of refreshment involves genuine concern, willingness to take risks, and persistence in service. It requires being alert to the needs of others and seeking to provide relief from the pressures that burden them.

STEPHEN HOPPER

Faithfulness in accomplishing routine tasks can help "unburden" a friend who must spend a great deal of time at a hospital. What a relief it is to come home to a lawn that is mysteriously mowed, to walk into a clean house, to find polished shoes and mended clothes in the closet, or to see that one's house plants are alive and cared for.

Carry each other's burdens, and in this way you will fulfill the law of Christ.

GALATIANS 6:2

52

Although it is important to remember the "firsts"—the first birthday, the first Christmas, the first anniversary—after a loved one's death, life goes on after the "firsts." We need to keep remembering our friend's need.

CANDY COOPER

An individual is never more Christ-like than when full of compassion for those who are down, needy, discouraged, or forgotten. How terribly essential is our commitment to encouragement!

CHARLES SWINDOLL

Many of us don't realize that suffering and grief take place over a long period of time and that the pain may worsen before it gets better. A true friend will be there for the long haul.

JAN DRAVECKY

One of our friends developed his own style of showing he cared. He never gave up on taking time out for us. He regularly made "house calls," accompanied by a box of chocolates. If we wanted to talk, he listened.

ROSEMARY COOPER

$\mathcal{A}$ FRIEND

LISTENS,

LISTENS,

AND

LISTENS

When people suffer they may feel emotions they never felt before. They may ask questions they had never thought to ask. They may say things they never dared to say before. Through it all, they need someone who loves them enough to listen.

He who can no longer listen to his brother will soon no longer be listening to God either.

DIETRICH BONHOEFFER

Many times I felt so helpless and discouraged, but then, out of the blue, my friend would call. Mother to mother, heart to heart, she would listen. She would cry with me, encourage me, and she always told me what a great kid my son was.

SARA HINES

A listener is a treasure.

ROSEMARY COOPER

What do you do when a hurting friend says things that are irreverent—or worse? Rejoice! Not in your friend's impiety, but in the willingness to entrust her pain to you.

DAVE BIEBEL

A despairing man should have the devotion of his friends, even though he forsakes the fear of the Almighty.

JOB 6:14

A good listener asks the right questions—ones that delve beneath the surface and help a hurting friend understand and express deep thoughts and feelings:

- *We have talked about everyone else, how are you doing?*
- *What are you doing to cope? What are you doing for yourself?*
- *Is this . . . what you are feeling?*
- *Do you understand why you feel that way?*
- *That seems difficult for you. Would you like to talk about it more?*

A friend is a person with whom I may be sincere, before whom I may think out loud.

RALPH WALDO EMERSON

$\mathcal{A}$ friend listens intently—makes eye contact, leans forward, expresses agreement or nods—to whatever a hurting friend says, even if it's been said many times before.

$\mathcal{T}$ake a tip from nature—your ears aren't made to shut, but your mouth is!

FRIENDS

DON'T

HAVE

TO HAVE

ALL THE

ANSWERS

Three of Job's friends heard of all the trouble that had fallen on him. Each traveled from his own country—Eliphaz from Teman, Bildad from Shuah, Zophar from Naamath—and went together to Job to keep him company and comfort him. When they first caught sight of him, they couldn't believe what they saw—they hardly recognized him! They cried out in lament, ripped their robes, and dumped dirt on their heads as a sign of their grief. Then they sat with him on the ground. Seven days and nights they sat there without saying a word. They could see how rotten he felt, how deeply he was suffering.

JOB 2:11-13 (the message)

A bit of advice: Say nothing often.

We are a "teller" society. We have never discovered the power of the ear. When someone tells us his/her problems we think we must have an answer. If we have no answer, we . . . either give shallow answers or just run from the question.

DOUG MANNING

He who answers before listening—that is his folly and his shame.

PROVERBS 18:13

Perhaps to defend God's honor, or to try to make some sense of what has happened, or simply to put the whole thing in the past, most would-be comforters are convinced that something must be said.

DAVE BIEBEL

Even a fool is thought wise if he keeps silent, and discerning if he holds his tongue.

PROVERBS 17:28

ENCOURAGEMENT
IS A TWO-WAY
STREET: FRIENDS
NOT ONLY
GIVE
ENCOURAGEMENT,
BUT RECEIVE IT
GRACIOUSLY.

Not only did my teenage son have cancer, but he developed spinal meningitis and slipped into a coma. When he awoke, he had lost his sight, hearing, and was bedridden. Yet he was so accepting of these terrible trials. In his blindness, he spoke of heavenly places, of seeing familiar faces and special angels. He was indeed in spiritual company. He was a hero to us all.

SARA HINES

Each of you received a spiritual gift. God has shown you his grace in giving you different gifts. And you are like servants who are responsible for using God's gifts. So be good servants and use your gifts to serve each other.

1 PETER 4:10 (icb)

During Dave's hospitalizations, we received more thoughtful gifts of flowers and fruit baskets than we could possibly use. So one day we loaded up a push cart with flowers and fruit, and Dave took off down the hall with them, his I.V. trailing behind him. You should have seen the expressions on people's faces when an ex-major leaguer rolled into their rooms with his flower cart. It was healing for us to be able to share with others.

JAN DRAVECKY

At times I receive the most encouragement by giving encouragement to others.

ROSEMARY COOPER

When I was a nineteen-year-old college student I learned that I would be a patient at a *children's* hospital. The last thing I wanted was to be treated as a child, but during each of my treatments I sat in a big toy room all afternoon. I was surrounded by Barbie dolls, crayons, Lincoln Logs, and some of the greatest heroes I have ever met. Through their unwavering valor in facing something as big as cancer, those little—often baldheaded—kids gave me a very special gift. They inspired me to be courageous and strong. As only children can, they enlivened my faith and trust in God.

MELANIE COOPER

I met my fiancée, Melanie, while she was battling cancer. Her strength in the midst of her trials was an encouragement to me. Her strength in the face of pain changed my life forever. It was impossible for me to think that someone in that much pain could manage a brilliant smile on a daily basis.

BRIAN NEWHOUSE

No matter if the mountains were so high and hard to climb, or if the sun did not shine, my daughter knew that Jesus was the answer. She has inspired me. My whole life has changed as I daily refocus my thoughts and actions with the Lord as my Savior.

LANE COOPER,
FATHER OF A CANCER PATIENT

... I want us to help each other with the faith that we have. Your faith will help me, and my faith will help you.

ROMANS 1:12 (icb)

Friends

SPEAK

WORDS OF

ENCOURAGEMENT

AND

COMFORT

The world is full of discouragers. We have a Christian duty to encourage one another. Many a time a word of praise or thanks or appreciation or cheer has kept a man on his feet. Blessed is the man who speaks such a word.

WILLIAM BARCLAY

The right word spoken at the right time is as beautiful as gold apples in a silver bowl.

PROVERBS 25:11 (icb)

WHAT YOU CAN SAY TO A SUFFERING FRIEND:

Can I give you a hug?

Can I pray for you right now?

The Lord is speaking to me through you and your situation.

    Can I tell you how?

It's okay to tell me you hurt. You don't have to be strong for me.

When you're ready to talk about that, I'll be here.

Words of comfort, skillfully administered, are the oldest therapy known to man.

LOUIS NIZER

TOP TEN BURDENSOME BLOOPERS

Words of understanding and comfort are precious to those who suffer, but it is sometimes hard to know what to say. When we're at a loss for words, we say whatever comes to mind, and the bloopers that result often wound those who hurt. So take a look at these "bloopers" and see if you may be offending when you want to comfort.

1. *Let me know if there is anything I can do to help! (Then please wait around for my answer.)*

2. *Why didn't you call and tell me what you needed? (Because I couldn't lift my head off the pillow.)*

3. *This must be God's will for your life. (Did He tell you that?)*

4. *I know what you must be going through. (You've lost your hair, too?)*

5. *Remember, time heals all wounds. (I hope that isn't why time has no end.)*

6. So, what are your chances? (Better than yours for "Encourager of the Year.")

7. Things could be worse. (Please don't elaborate!)

8. Look on the bright side. (I would if I knew what it was.)

9. You have the same thing as my aunt, but she died. (Thank you so much for sharing that.)

10. It's so wonderful that you will see Jesus before the rest of us! (Don't be so sure.)

Let thy speech be better than silence, or be silent.

DIONYSIUS THE ELDER

Let your speech always be with grace, seasoned [as it were] with salt, so that you may know how you should respond to each person.
COLOSSIANS 4:6 (NASB)

Nobody cares how much you know until they know how much you care.

DAVID JEREMIAH

FRIENDS

GIVE

ADVICE

SPARINGLY

There's definitely a place for counsel and advice from friends and family, but it is so important to give it without strings attached. Please don't feel rejected if a hurting friend doesn't follow your advice. Dave's parents fought for Dave to keep his arm, but once Dave decided the arm had to go, they supported us in it. That meant so much to us.

JAN DRAVECKY

Advice is like snow—the softer it falls, the deeper it goes.

People who are suffering may need advice, but they also need to make their own decisions, even if they turn out to be the "wrong" ones. We are each responsible to live our lives, not the lives of others.

DAVE AND JAN DRAVECKY

When you talk, do not say harmful things. But say what people need—words that will help others become stronger. Then what you say will help those who listen to you.

EPHESIANS 4:29 (icb)

$\mathcal{F}$riends need to know when to let go. No one stays in a place of suffering and need forever. Eventually people grow to a point that they need their friends simply as friends, not as fixers. Not all friendships survive that transition.

DAVE AND JAN DRAVECKY

$\mathcal{T}$here is a time for everything, and a season for every activity under heaven: . . . a time to heal, . . . a time to weep and a time to laugh, a time to mourn and a time to dance, . . . a time to keep and a time to throw away, a time to tear and a time to mend, a time to be silent and a time to speak.

ECCLESIASTES 3:1–7

Friends

FIND

WAYS TO

TOUCH

YOUR

HEART

Encouragement came to us in unexpected ways. We would come home after a day at the hospital with our teenage son to find notes of encouragement in our mailbox. His friends often left flowers and notes of love and encouragement to him on the front porch. At other times, pictures of our son and his friends that had been taken on camping trips and other outings were left taped to our front door. It was wonderful to be surprised by these touching expressions of love at the end of a long, painful day.

SARA HINES

It is not how much we do, but how much love we put into what we do.

MOTHER TERESA

When my wife was seriously ill and the doctors could not find the cause of her illness, someone gave me a tape of Andraé Crouch's great little chorus, "Through it all, I've learned to trust in Jesus, I've learned to trust in God." I played that song over and over until I wore out the tape. Music is one of God's most blessed gifts.

DAVID JEREMIAH

An anxious heart weighs a man down, but a kind word cheers him up.

PROVERBS 12:25

When my son was able to eat again, my dear sister-in-law made a turkey dinner—my son's favorite meal—just for him. He still couldn't eat regular solid food, so my husband, who kept a blender by Ryan's bedside, blended each part like baby food. It still had the great flavor he loved, and I don't know of a meal made with more love than that.

SARA HINES

Be encouraged in heart and united in love.

COLOSSIANS 2:2

A FRIEND

ENCOURAGES

THROUGH

PRAYER

During one of the deepest, darkest times in my life a fellow pastor called me just to say, "David, I want you to know I love you, and I know you are going through some hurt. I want you to know I'm here if you need me. I want to pray with you." And he prayed with me on the phone. He called me every week for several weeks with a word of encouragement. He poured courage into my heart.

DAVID JEREMIAH

The prayer of a righteous man is powerful and effective.

JAMES 5:16

A friend once said, "Through my suffering of the past few years, many people have promised to pray for me. But you were the only one who sat down next to me and actually prayed with me. I cannot begin to tell you how much that meant to me."

AMANDA SORENSON

Be joyful in hope, patient in affliction, faithful in prayer.

ROMANS 12:12

From the day my tumor was discovered, I prayed daily for my surgeon. Just before my surgery, he came to my bedside. His face and body were masked in mint-green surgery garb; only his smiling eyes were visible. At that moment, when uncertainty filled my heart, he said that he was praying for me. The comfort of that one phrase nurtured my strength.

MELANIE COOPER

A friend will strengthen you with his prayers, bless you with his love, and encourage you with his hope.

A FRIEND

SPEAKS

THROUGH

ACTS OF

KINDNESS

One of my friends baked chocolate chip cookies for me every week during a period of grief.

DEE MARTZ

Words, although important, were not nearly as important as the acts of love and kindness that were shown to us. Words spoken are exactly that. Things done speak much louder and last much longer.

DWAYNE POTTEIGER

*J*esus modeled a practical brand of love. His was a love that ministered to his disciples' pressing needs.

- Jesus was concerned about their families, homes, and health.
- Jesus was willing to take time for people in need even though he was engaged in a busy ministry.
- Jesus provided faithful support in the spiritual battle by intercessory prayer.
- Jesus extended complete forgiveness, even when it seemed undeserved.
- Jesus humbly served his followers, exemplified in his washing their feet.

So it is with us. If we are to love our brothers and sisters as Jesus commanded, we must learn to express a practical love for the whole person. It must be the kind of love our Master has shown to us.

WILLIAM FLETCHER

$\mathcal{G}$ive your friend a haircut, manicure, facial, or new hairstyle. A fresh look, and knowing that someone still cares to help him or her look good can be an encouragement. Of course, if these things aren't your personal forte, hire someone else to do the job!

$\mathcal{A}$ brother or sister in Christ might need clothes or might need food. And you say to him, "God be with you! I hope you stay warm and get plenty to eat." You say this, but you do not give that person the things he needs. Unless you help him, your words are worth nothing.

JAMES 2:15-16 (icb)

FRIENDS

HELP OUT

IN THE

DAILY

GRIND

When a family's routine is upset, dirty laundry piles up even faster than the mail! A family doesn't soon forget the person who quietly gathers the dirty laundry and brings it back, folded, ironed, ready to wear.

Offering good advice may be noble and grand, but it's not the same as a helping hand.

The thought of picking up the phone and getting information or arranging business can be overwhelming. So make phone calls for your friend—to cancel the newspaper, to make appointments, to hassle with the insurance company, to check on test results, to find out a child's sporting event or rehearsal schedule—whatever your friend may need.

If anyone . . . sees his brother in need but has no pity on him, how can the love of God be in him?

1 JOHN 3:17

If you provide meals for a friend, send food in containers that don't need to be returned, and put a note to that effect with the meal. And if your friend is receiving meals from others, take the responsibility to return the dishes to the rightful owner. Returning dishes is a job hurting people don't need. Meals are a blessing, but meals with no follow-up work are a double blessing!

Serve wholeheartedly, as if you were serving the Lord, not men.

EPHESIANS 6:7

Help with the paperwork! Insurance forms and taxes are a major headache—even if you're healthy. If you're qualified, handle the insurance filing or see to it that tax deadlines are met.

❧

A good friend is like a tube of toothpaste—comes through in a tight squeeze.

During a time of adversity or crisis, driving from one place to another can become a burden. Offer to:

- Take a friend's children to lessons, sports practices, and appointments
- Drive your friend to the hospital for treatments or tests
- Drive your friend to doctor's appointments
- Drive family members to the hospital for visits
- Pick up out-of-town family at the airport

Your faithfulness will make life a little easier for your friend.

For three months, we were at the hospital for thirteen to fourteen hours a day. Neighbors took turns walking our dog who was home alone.

SARA HINES

FRIENDS

DON'T

ALWAYS

ACT

ALONE

A community BBQ and auction was held to raise funds for our daughter's battle against cancer. We had been feeling very weary, alone, and uncertain, and we were shocked to see how many people cared about our trial. We live in a community of only four hundred, but eight hundred people came. That sunny day was an encouragement to us. It showed that people were willing to come alongside and cheer us on.

ROSEMARY COOPER

May the God who gives endurance and encouragement give you a spirit of unity among yourselves as you follow Christ Jesus.

ROMANS 15:5

There are many ways to work together to lighten the load for those who suffer. Some efforts require but a few minutes to set up and an individual commitment to follow through. Others require more extensive planning and weeks of cooperative work. Consider these ideas, and see what you can do.

When we were at a very low point, a group of friends who cared about us arranged a retreat to help us regain perspective and set boundaries so that we could move on. A year later, we gathered together again to follow up and look more toward the future.

Neighbors or a church community can set up a schedule to bring prepared meals to a family when they arrive home following long days at the hospital.

Five of Dave's friends, who lived all over the country, set up a schedule to call Dave on a regular basis. For one year, Dave heard from one of these friends every few weeks.

One family was building their own home when catastrophic illness struck. Their friends finished painting the interior and installed all the wood trim, so the home was completed when the family member was ready to come home to recuperate.

A group of friends may pool their resources to purchase a scarf wardrobe or a hairpiece for a woman who loses her hair from chemotherapy or radiation.

DAVE AND JAN DRAVECKY

FRIENDS

CARE

FOR THE

WHOLE

FAMILY

People often overlook the needs of those who are close to a cancer patient. Yet those loving caregivers suffer, too. Be sure to ask them how they are doing, not just how the patient is doing.

I want to express my deepest thanks for your love and concern. You have been a real blessing in my wife's life. No one seems to see beyond me and my cancer—to see a whole family in turmoil during these trials. My wife has truly been kept by the power of the Holy Spirit.

A CANCER PATIENT IN A LETTER TO HIS FRIEND

When a sibling or parent is seriously ill, it's easy to overlook the personal needs of young children. The gift of something as simple as a coloring book, new crayons or markers, or colorful stickers can help brighten a child's lonely heart. It says to the child, "In the midst of all the busyness and confusion, you are not forgotten. I care about what is important to you."

$\mathcal{M}$en whose loved ones are suffering have a need for encouragement, too. Although they may have to "be strong" and keep on working to support their family, they need support. They need other men to reach out to them. Perhaps an invitation for breakfast or a cup of coffee can help a man "open up" and talk about all the worrisome things that are happening to his family.

CANDY COOPER

$\mathcal{W}$e all need the fuel of love and relationship to continue growing and healing.

DR. JOHN TOWNSEND

Frequent hospital treatments are a burden in any situation, but when one has a family of school-age children, they can be a nightmare. One cancer patient shares, "A family took care of our children every day after school until we returned home after treatments at the hospital. It was a tremendous relief to know that our children were cared for and safe."

He took a little child and had him stand among them. Taking him in his arms, he said to them, "Whoever welcomes one of these little children in my name welcomes me."

MARK 9:36-37

It's not just the immediate family that needs special attention, it's the extended family, too. Perhaps you can help keep out-of-town family members in touch by sending periodic e-mail or fax updates. Or, if those family members come to visit, perhaps you can provide a place for them to stay.

Friends used their frequent flyer miles to purchase tickets so that our whole family could visit with out-of-town family members during the holidays.

DWAYNE POTTEIGER

$\mathcal{A}$ FRIEND

KNOWS THE

COMFORT OF

A LOVING

TOUCH

Everyone was meant to share God's all-abiding love and care;
He saw that we would need to know a way to let these feelings show . . . so
God made hugs.

JILL WOLF

My pastor and many of my dad's friends give us big "daddy
hugs."

MICHELLE VAN HORN

When I was receiving news about Dave's condition, it was so comforting for someone to hold my hand or place an arm around my shoulders. Just that simple touch helped me know that I wasn't alone.

JAN DRAVECKY

Quite often God entrusts His great love to the gentle touch of a human hand, the familiar sound of a human voice.

KIM JONES

Scented lotion can be a good gift for a patient. Not only is the lotion soothing to the skin and the fragrance pleasing to the sense of smell, the touch of applying it is comforting and healing as well.

One day when I was hurting physically, Dave's mom gave me a backrub. It felt so good. It meant so much more because I knew that she wasn't normally a physically affectionate person. That backrub was a real gift.

JAN DRAVECKY

Make an appointment for your friend to receive a massage. A massage can be comforting, invigorating, and refreshing to a person who has been ill or under stress.

I long for the glow of a kindly heart and the grasp of a friendly hand.

J. B. O'REILLY

When you are hospitalized for cancer treatment, you experience so much negative touch—needle sticks, invasive pokes and prods, painful tests—that you begin to long for positive touch. A hug, a soft stroke on the head, a gentle hand in yours become more important than ever.

SUSAN STRONG

A man with leprosy came to him and begged him on his knees, "If you are willing, you can make me clean." Filled with compassion, Jesus reached out his hand and touched the man. "I am willing," he said.

MARK 1:40-41

FRIENDS

ENCOURAGE

THROUGH

THE

WRITTEN

WORD

Some of our friends put together an album that was filled with notes and letters that expressed their love to us. The stories they shared of how we had touched their lives was deeply moving.

DWAYNE AND RHONDA POTTEIGER

Written encouragement comes directly from the heart, uninterrupted and unhindered. That's why it's so powerful.

DAVID JEREMIAH

One of our pastors, Brent Allen, wrote out a psalm and sent it to us every day for a period of two weeks before and after my surgery.

DAVE AND JAN DRAVECKY

For everything that was written in the past was written to teach us, so that through endurance and the encouragement of the Scriptures we might have hope.

ROMANS 15:4

Unlike the spoken word, written words of encouragement can be read repeatedly whenever comfort is needed. A woman once received a thank-you note for a sympathy card. It read, "So many people at church told me they were sorry my grandmother had died, but you were the only one who sent a card, who wrote something to me."

So, when they were sent away, they went down to Antioch; and having gathered the congregation together, they delivered the letter. And when they had read it, they rejoiced because of its encouragement.

ACTS 15:30–31 (NASB)

We had a large basket that nearly overflowed with the many thoughtful cards and letters people sent to us. Just seeing that overflowing basket reminded us that people really cared for us—not just while our son was sick, but during the months of healing that followed his death.

CANDY COOPER

We were blessed by the cards people sent. An eighth grade class "adopted" us. They prayed for us and sent cards and letters that always seemed to arrive at our lowest points. Another friend sent us cards every week. The funny ones were the best.

SANDRA VAN HORN

When a person is suffering physically, it is easy to feel unlovable, even worthless. Write out a "love alphabet" for your friend. For every letter of the alphabet, choose an adjective that describes your friend. Here's a sample:

A: Misty is authentic. (Not phony)

I: Misty is insightful. (Sees with more than her eyes)

F: Misty is fervent. (Intensely devoted)

M: Misty is a mother's delight. (I'm proud of her)

Got the idea? Bless a friend with your words.

DAVE BIEBEL

Excerpt from a letter a patient received from her doctor: "It certainly is great to hear that you are doing so well.... You certainly are an inspiration to me as well as, I am sure, to all those with whom you come in contact." To think that a busy physician would take the time to write to a patient!

A FRIEND

SHARES

MEMORIES,

AND HELPS

MAKE

NEW ONES

$\mathcal{I}$ am a husband and father with two young children, and my diagnosis is terminal. Friends gave our family one-year passes to a favorite local attraction so that we could spend time doing nothing more than having fun together. Their gift helps us build family memories that will be so important in the years ahead.

DWAYNE POTTEIGER

When you give a memory-building gift, include a disposable camera and photo album to record the event.

Don't be afraid to talk with your friend about the family member who is ill or has died. Your friend will tell you if he or she doesn't want to talk. Being able to share precious memories that are close to your friend's heart may be a healing blessing.

It was a real blessing to hear friends and family express their love and memories of our son at his memorial service. Hearing others describe what they treasured about our son and how he ministered to them helped us work through our grief.

CANDY COOPER

Some dear friends put together a beautiful album of photos and newspaper clippings that chronicled my career through my initial diagnosis, comeback, and eventual retirement from baseball. That was an awesome gift of love. Jan and I had clippings, too, but they were in a box somewhere. It meant so much to be able to look back and remember the journey we had been on.

DAVE AND JAN DRAVECKY

Live a life of love just as Christ loved us.

EPHESIANS 5:2 (icb)

Make Special Occasions Memorable

Just because a person is ill doesn't change the fact that he or she is still a parent, husband, wife, son, or daughter who wants to bless his or her loved ones on special occasions. Perhaps you can be the friend who will:

- Make sure that a wife receives a bouquet of flowers from her husband on her birthday or on Valentine's Day.
- Arrange, on your friend's behalf, for a special dinner to celebrate a wedding anniversary.
- Select, have your friend sign, and mail a Mother's Day or Father's Day card (to the parents as well as to the spouse).
- Write out a card or note that a friend who is unable to write dictates to you.
- Plan and supervise a birthday party for a child.
- Faithfully attend a child's sporting, musical, academic, or dramatic events when the parent can't.

- Go as a "surrogate parent" to an awards or graduation ceremony for a child, and videotape the event.
- Purchase tickets to a family member's favorite sporting event or concert as a gift from the sick person.
- With your friend's help, shop for Christmas gifts, then wrap and send them.
- Help your friend maintain family holiday traditions such as preparing a particular food (baking cookies or a special kind of cake) or participating in a traditional activity (helping decorate Easter Eggs).

FRIENDS

CELEBRATE

THE

MILESTONES

Our church had an "Off-Treatment" party for our son. We had a reason to celebrate, and the outpouring of love—more than two hundred people attended—touched us deeply. It was a great encouragement.

CANDY COOPER

Many of us are avid sports fans who invest money, time, energy, and emotion into cheering our favorite teams on to victory. This enthusiastic encouragement is considered an advantage for the home team. Why? The presence of people who feel for us and with us helps bring out the best in us. The cheering fans at sports events are saying to the players, "We care. We think you're great. We're proud of you." And the players respond.

LOIS MOWDAY RABEY

A FRIEND

HELPS YOU

LOOK

BEYOND

TODAY

Even in the midst of the battle, life is more than cancer. Yet it is difficult to maintain any semblance of normal life when people express concern only about your cancer and treatments. Ask about the rest of life too—other people, events, thoughts, hopes, and dreams.

BRIAN NEWHOUSE

In the middle of cancer treatments, it's hard to think beyond just what has to be done to get through each day. It was great when friends took the initiative to include our family in their family fun and adventures. On one memorable day we went racing at "Malibu Raceway."

DWAYNE POTTEIGER

Friends gave us a cruise to enjoy after my husband's treatments were completed. That gift gave us something to look forward to during those difficult days.

SANDRA VAN HORN

All of us need encouragement—somebody to believe in us. To reassure and reinforce us. To help us pick up the pieces and go on. To provide us with increased determination in spite of the odds.

CHARLES SWINDOLL

$\mathcal{A}$ few days after Dad died, a friend took me to a movie—just so I could laugh. Later, a friend invited my brother to play golf with him on Dad's birthday. That helped him look forward to the day.

MICHELLE VAN HORN

$\mathcal{T}$he LORD will guide you always; he will satisfy your needs in a sun-scorched land and will strengthen your frame. You will be like a well-watered garden, like a spring whose waters never fail.

ISAIAH 58:11

$\mathcal{A}$ FRIEND

GIVES HOPE

BY SHARING

THE SOURCE

OF HOPE

On the day before we left for a much-needed family vacation, an arrangement of red roses was delivered to our home. The card read, "A rose for each of you. I love you. Jesus." I read the card and cried and cried and cried. It was more than an expression of love from another person; it was an affirmation that God was still with us, that He still loved us, that He had heard our desperate cry for one final "family memory" vacation with our son.

CANDY COOPER

Every true friend is a glimpse of God.

LUCY LARCOM

One family sent us a balloon bouquet with a reminder from Luke 1:37: "Nothing is impossible with God." I don't know how, but that bouquet stayed inflated for twenty months, serving as a constant, visible reminder that God was with us in our situation. It helped us keep our focus on Him.

CANDY COOPER

It is an awesome, challenging thought: The Lord comes to us in our friends. What we do and are to them is an expression of what we are to Him.

LLOYD JOHN OGILVIE

By searching for and telling others of the many "little miracles" God has done through my battle with cancer, I have been encouraged. Through my efforts to share my story with others, I have realized that God will never abandon His beloved children.

MELANIE COOPER

But those who hope in the LORD will renew their strength.

ISAIAH 40:31

Our hope is in the Promise, not the possibilities. Although I can have hope for better health, what I need to rest in is the promise that God will sustain me in all circumstances and provide me a residence in His Presence, no matter what.

JIM ARNOLDI

Good intentions and my strength, resources, and mercy may be found wanting, but God's love has no limits.

KIM JONES

When we face suffering, strengthening one another with the true hope Jesus offers is one of the most important things we can do. We can do this in many little ways that make a difference:

- Many times when Dave was too weak or weary to read on his own, I read the Scriptures to him. They continually reminded us of our true source of hope.

- Giving a cassette of praise music is a beautiful way to lift one's spirits heavenward.

- Placing a picture of Jesus where the patient can see it helps remind him or her of Jesus' faithful presence.

- It may be possible to decorate the patient's room with favorite Scripture verses lettered on poster board.

JAN DRAVECKY

Therefore we do not lose heart. Though outwardly we are wasting away, yet inwardly we are being renewed day by day. For our light and momentary troubles are achieving for us an eternal glory that far outweighs them all. So we fix our eyes not on what is seen, but on what is unseen. For what is seen is temporary, but what is unseen is eternal.

2 CORINTHIANS 4:16–18

DAVE DRAVECKY'S OUTREACH OF HOPE

On the Sistine Chapel is one of Michaelangelo's most famous paintings. God is reaching down from heaven with hand extended to touch the outstretched hand of man. The natural human response to pain and suffering is often to do just the opposite—to recoil and retreat. Thus the very thing we need most, the love and intimacy of God, can seem furthest from us.

Through Dave and Jan's battles with cancer and depression, they realized just how necessary love and encouragement are. At times they experienced the blessing of encouragement—God's touch through the love and actions of people. Their desire is to gently and lovingly pick up the weary arm and lift it heavenward.

To this end they have established Dave Dravecky's Outreach of Hope, a ministry dedicated to offering hope and encouragement through Jesus Christ to those who suffer from cancer or amputation. This mission is accomplished through prayer support, personal contact, correspondence, resource referral, and the gift of encouraging literature. Inquiries may be directed to Dave Dravecky's Outreach of Hope, 13840 Gleneagle Drive, Colorado Springs, CO 80921, or e-mail info@outreachofhope.org

ACKNOWLEDGING THE PEOPLE WHO SHARED THEIR STORIES

We would like to thank each individual and family who so graciously shared their stories with us.

JIM ARNOLDI was diagnosed with a rare form of terminal leiomyosarcoma in 1989. Since that time he has undergone surgery sixteen times, endured kidney failure and weekly dialysis, all the while continuing to manage his lumber business. At this writing, Jim, his wife Carole, and son Chris are preparing to retire and move to Georgia.

DAVE BIEBEL and his wife have had four children. His first son, Jonathan, died from a rare metabolic disorder at age three. A second son, Christopher, has been diagnosed with the same illness but currently is doing well. Dave honestly shares his story in his book *Jonathan, You Left Too Soon.* Dave has also written *If God Is So Good—Why Do I Hurt So Bad?* and *Helping Those Who Hurt.*

MARK AND CANDY COOPER live in Texas and are the parents of four children. Their third son, Adam, was diagnosed with leukemia when he was fifteen months old. His baby sister was able to provide perfectly matched bone marrow for a transplant, but it was not successful. In September 1995, when he was five years old, Adam died at home, surrounded by his family.

MELANIE COOPER is a college student from Michigan who has battled a cancerous desmoid tumor in her right arm. She and her parents, LANE AND ROSEMARY COOPER, lost her younger brother to a brain tumor when he was four years old. Melanie is presently doing well and will soon be married to BRIAN NEWHOUSE.

HEATHER GROUNDS is a college student from Colorado who was diagnosed with synovial sarcoma in her right leg. She has completed surgery and chemotherapy and is currently cancer free.

ROGER AND SARA HINES lost their only child, twenty-year-old Ryan, to lymphoma in September of 1994. For several months during his illness, Ryan was confined to bed, unable to see or hear. God continues to be their source of strength and comfort as they deal with the loss of their son.

DAVID JEREMIAH is the pastor of Shadow Mountain Community Church in San Diego, California. He has been diagnosed with lymphoma and is now in remission. David has authored several books, including the recently released *Power of Encouragement*.

KIM JONES has served on the pastoral staff of a church, has worked in the medical field, and is on staff at the Outreach of Hope. She walked closely with her best friend through her battle with a terminal brain tumor.

Four months after they married, DEE MARTZ'S second husband was diagnosed with leukemia. He experienced a very brief remission but died eight months after their wedding day. Dee is currently a grief counselor and has married David Martz, an oncologist.

In 1992, DWAYNE POTTEIGER was diagnosed with anaplastic astrocytoma, an aggressive brain cancer that has a survival rate of only three to four years. Dwayne has since outlived that prognosis and resigned his staff position with a large church in California to move to Colorado with his wife, RHONDA, and their two young children. Although still in the midst of the battle, he is presently on staff with Kingdom Building Ministries.

PRISSILLY THE CLOWN is also known as Sharon Stuck. She has a balloon and entertainment business, is a Christian speaker, and regularly visits with patients at local hospitals. She is currently dealing with her father's death due to cancer and her mother's recent cancer diagnosis.

At age seventeen, SUSAN STRONG was diagnosed with a rare form of Hodgkins disease. She has been in remission for fourteen years and has been a great encouragement to her younger sister who was also diagnosed with cancer at age seventeen. Susan now encourages others as a staff member at the Outreach of Hope.

SANDRA AND MICHELLE VAN HORN are the wife and daughter of Mike Van Horn, who died from lung cancer in 1996. Mike also leaves behind a son, Toby. Mike was on staff with Youth for Christ for thirteen years. Through his life and death, he left behind an incredible legacy.

We also thank the staff at the Outreach of Hope for their ideas and stories.

CREDITS